MYSTIC'S M

The spells in this book are mainly from
own personal collection from my 15 year
They are in no particular order as I thought it best this way.
Enjoy and always use responsibly, never use a spell against
another person.
The poems and other magical texts are also from the public
domain.
Mystic.

FRIENDSHIP CANDLE SPELL

You Will Need:

*Pink Candle

*Good Luck/Friendship Oil

*Pink silk Ribbon

*White Silk Ribbon

Cast the Circle, arrange altar, Invoke Goddess, and God. You will want to anoint the pink with Good Luck oil all the while thinking of the friends you want to make. Imagine yourself laughing with them, going out with them. Really see yourself with them.

After your candle has been anointed, you may light it. At this point, you may call out the things that are important to you in a friend: honesty, trust, open mindedness, humour, whatever.

As you light the candle, see the flame as being the energy that burns between any two close friends. When this is completed, take your two pieces of silk ribbon and weave them together. Simply winding them around each other will do. While you do this, think of bringing that friend closer to you.

This binding process is reminiscent of pagan handfasting rituals. You are binding that friend to you, making them loyal to you, a way any good friend should be. You do not want to bind a specific person to you, as that kind of magic is harmful since is harms the other person's free will. Only bind the idea of the perfect friend to you.

Once you have done this, tie the ribbon to the base of your candle as best as you can. The candle's light is a beacon to bring friendship to you and another person. When this is done, you may wish to sit and meditate on the spell that you have just cast, sending your energies out to bring that perfect friend to you. When you feel that your spell has been completed, then it has. Let your candle burn all the way out and release your circle, thanking the Goddess and
the God.

A SPELL TO BREAK A BAD HABIT.

This is a very simple candle spell that can be used to break any bad habit.

This should be performed during a waning moon.

You will need: A candle (black is the best colour for this)

Pen and paper

Write down the habit that you wish to be rid of on the piece of paper.

Now light the candle, and stare into the flame as you clear your mind of all thought.

Take the paper and burn it with the candle, while chanting:

With this cleansing flame, I banish you from my life So mote it be.

Once you have done this, it's time to formulate a new intent, which you will write down on another piece of paper.

Make sure your new intent is positive, and written in present tense.

Here are a few examples:

To stop smoking: I am a healthy non-smoker

To stop procrastinating: I feel motivated to get things done

To stop biting your nails: My nails are healthy and strong

Every morning, for the next 21 days, write down your new intent three times on a fresh piece of paper.

A SPELL TO BANISH NEGATIVE ENERGY.

This incantation will spiritually cleanse a place, and banish unwanted energies.

It is very useful for purifying a place of ritual before creating a circle, and also to remove remaining energy from unpleasant visitors after a ritual.

You can even use this as a hasty defense to ward off malevolent spirits.

Just say the following incantation aloud or in your head, while drawing a pentagram in the air – imagine the pentagram to be made of bright white light. At the end of the incantation, let the white light escape in order to enlighten and purify every corner of the area to be cleaned.

"In these names that are above all others, the name of the great lady and powerful Lord, I hunt by seed, flower and fruit of evil, I cast a spell on them with power and purity, whether constrained by chains or returned to darkness, they may never disturb the servants of the gods."

PROTECTION AGAINST HARMFUL SPIRITS.

If you find yourself being attacked or otherwise influenced by an otherworldly spirit or entity, you must seek protection.

This is a three-stage process to rid yourself of the unwanted beings and protect yourself.

1. Protection

If you can, acquire one or more of the following gemstones:

Black Tourmaline
Agate Bloodstone
Emerald Labradorite
Black Onyx
Peridot Emerald

These are crystals that protect you from harmful spirits and psychic intrusion. Black Tourmaline may be the most effective, but any of them would work.
If you can find orgonite containing one of these stones, that would be even more effective.
The next step will be to surround yourself with a shield of protective light.
This comes from within, and you can conjure it up yourself through meditation. Begin each day with sitting down in a quiet space for five minutes, visualizing a bright bubble of light around you, reaching about an arm's length away from your body.
Make it any colour you feel comfortable with. Repeat the following words:
"I surround myself with a shield of protection. I am safe within my space."
Feel the light emanating from you, growing brighter with each deep breath.
It is strong and controlled, vibrating at a high frequency.
No evil spirit can penetrate this force field.
Finally, ask your spirit guides, guardian angels and the God and Goddess to protect you.

2. Cleansing

You will then need to cleanse the space where you sense the negative intrusion. If it follows you around, use these methods around your body. If you can, find some Palo Santo (available for a few dollars on Etsy or eBay) – it is a holy wood from the Amazon burned by Shamans to drive out evil spirits and unwanted energies.
Otherwise, you can use sage, sandalwood or frankincense.
Sprinkle sea salt around the area.
Say words like the following, over and over as you cleanse your space:
"Any unwanted spirits and entities, please leave now. Any evil or negative energies or presences, please leave this space. You don't

belong here. I am sending you home. Go back whence you came. Please leave NOW. Only light and healing energy is allowed in this room. Thank you."

Repeat these or similar words until you feel satisfied.

3. Communication Follow steps 1 and 2.

If they don't work, you must try to communicate with the spirit.

This can be dangerous, so follow the instructions carefully.

Cast a protective circle. Sprinkle sea salt over it for extra protection.

Wear or carry your gemstones or orgonite.

Ask them to protect you.

Activate your protective light shield as per step 1.

Then you may speak to the spirit. Say something along the lines of:

"Spirit who presently resides here. I am protected and you cannot harm me.

I address you with the utmost respect.

I do not know your reasons for being here, but you are intruding on my/our live(s), and there is nothing for you here. I am asking you to please leave.

Go back whence you came. Go home, where you will be at peace. Thank you." When you're ready, close your circle.

Keep your gemstones or orgonite near you as often as you can. Whenever you feel like there might be a negative presence, take deep breaths (which strengthens your aura), try to remain calm, visualize the light bubble around you, and ask your guides/angels to stay near and keep you safe.

If this still doesn't work, you should contact a psychic for assistance.

PROTECTION SPELL AGAINST NEGATIVITY AND PSYCHIC VAMPIRES.

This is a white magic spell which will help protect you against negative people. It will protect you from all negative actions against you: jealousy, gossip, verbal attacks, and even sorcery. Most importantly, it will protect you against psychic vampires who can literally suck the life-energy out of you.
For this spell against negative people, you will need:
A picture of yourself
4 blue candles and one white candle
A few drops of essential oil for your astrological sign
Sage incense
3 acacia leaves
3 black tourmaline stones

Casting the Spell Against Negative People and Psychic Vampires.
Purify yourself by washing your hands in a bowl of water that contains a drop of your essential oil.
Prepare the circle by placing the blue candles on each cardinal point, and the white candle in front of you.
Put the incense to the left of the white candle, and the acacia leaves and the tourmaline stones to the right of the candle.
Place your photo in front of the candle.
Cast the circle, and light all the candles and the incense.
Take your photo and pass it over the incense three times, and as you do so, imagine the incense purifying this representation of you, clearing away all negativity which has been sent your way by these negative people and psychic vampires.
Take the acacia leaves and the black tourmaline in your hands, and recite the following incantation five times:
"I invoke thee, Aradia, goddess of protection and healing, protect me and keep me safe, Now and forever, Thank you."
See a circle of white light forming around you, which psychic vampires and negative people cannot penetrate.
Extinguish the candle and close the circle, but let the incense burn until the end.

PROTECTION TIPS AND TALISMANS FOR WICCANS.

There are many basic techniques of protection that don't require any rituals or incantations.

These things are so easy and effective that all Wiccans need to know about them:

Salt – A circle of salt around an area prevents negative entities and demons from crossing into it.

You can make a line of salt along a door or windowsill to make it impassable.

Iron – Iron symbolizes the pure will, and repels evil.

This is why Wiccans sometimes put an iron object in the entrance of their homes to deter unwanted visitors.

Three iron nails driven into the frame of a door or window (one at each bottom corner and one in the top middle) block malevolent spirits from passing.

It is also said that most spirits are unable to cross a railway line because the iron forms an impenetrable wall for them.

They must instead use a bridge or a tunnel below ground.

Silver – This symbolizes the Moon and the Goddess, making silver jewellery easy to enchant to make talismans of protection.

A silver pentacle is a powerful protection even without a spell.

The Pentacle – the five-pointed star symbolizing the five elements can be traced almost anywhere as a powerful symbol of protection.

Light – Many lesser demons avoid bright places and attack only when it is dark. This, unfortunately, has no use against the demons of higher rank.

Fire – Some evil spirits fear fire, especially those spirits related to water or ice. In some cases, a single candle can be a protection.

Crystals – Four quartz crystals previously blessed by a witch can create a circle of protection very quickly.

Simply arrange them in a circle on the ground to create a circle that most spirits would find it hard to cross.

This circle can protect you, or instead it can be used to trap a spirit in the middle.

The circle is much stronger if the crystals are placed by the cardinal points. Gemstones – stones and gems have qualities useful in magic, and many are effective for protection.

Tiger's eye reflects negative energies to their source; Amethyst blocks manipulative spells and decreases the effect of harmful potions, magnetite can be used to entrap lesser demons, while opal can temporarily lock even higher demons, onyx, and obsidian capture and cancel various negative energies including those used in necromancy.

The mineral most often used by sorcerers is clear quartz, but it must be blessed or enchanted for it to be effective as protection.

Two apples and a knife – This is another very simple method to create a circle of protection.

An apple cut in half crosswise presents five areas containing its seeds as a natural pentacle! Deposited on the ground by the cardinal points, two half apples create a circle of temporary protection, which disappears when the apples are completely oxidized and have changed colour.

Incense – Some types of incense can make the air unbearable for bad spirits.

If you have a good quality incense, you can keep many of them away.

The most common protective incense types are sandalwood, patchouli, myrrh, frankincense, and sage.

Plants – Several herbs, spices and other plants used in Wicca have protective qualities.

Garlic repels creatures that drain their victims (thus everything that has a vampiric nature); saffron and thyme deter flying spirits that are associated with the wind; rosemary repels evil spirits associated with water;

Sage, when burnt, is very cleansing and intolerable to evil spirits.

Henbane and aconite violently repel demons, but they are very toxic plants so be careful when handling them!

Lilacs planted near a home will deter wandering spirits who come by chance (but they won't stop those who come with a clear goal in mind).

Branches of a thorny plant (such as a rose) placed along a door or windowsill will form a barrier as effective as a line of salt.

Finally, myrrh strengthens almost all spells and protective talismans.

The Athame – Although many Wiccans do not sharpen their Athame and never use it to cut anything, this knife is nevertheless a weapon, in addition to being a phallic symbol and thus a symbol of God.

An Athame which has been properly blessed can draw a circle of protection very quickly – point it in the air and draw the boundaries of the circle.

In addition, unlike any other blade, an Athame can hurt spirits and demons even though they have no physical body.

Broom – This is a symbol for cleansing, and a broom placed by the door will prevent weaker spirits from entering. If a particularly dangerous spirit enters the house, the broom will tend to fall to the ground as an alarm signal.

A SPELL TO DREAM OF THE FUTURE

Dream divination is the power to see the future and enhance clairvoyance through dreaming. To foresee an event in the future through a dream, try this powerful dream ritual.

Decide what subject your prophetic/psychic dream will be about:

*Does it involve you, or someone else?

*What is the subject you need information on? (Money, love, etc.)

*How far or near in the future do you wish to see?

*Do you have a specific question to ask, or just a general topic?

*How do you want the question answered- by a guide, symbols, emotions, etc.?

Once you are sure you know what exactly the prophetic dream should be, you can gather your items and prepare your working.

Lay out a square of pale blue cloth. In the middle, places a mixture of ash leaves, bay leaves, cinquefoil, heliotrope, holly, jasmine flowers, marigold flowers, mimosa, mugwort, onion, and/or yarrow (however many you can find).

Bring the corners towards the middle and tie it all together like a small bag with a string, ribbon, or piece of yarn. Then, on a white piece of paper, briefly explain what you need to see in the dream, using the guideline above to tell the main ideas/questions you need prophecies about. Place the herbal bag and the note beneath your pillow, and make sure you record your dream in a notebook or journal as soon as you awake, so you do not forget it. Use what you learn to prepare you for the future.

NEW JOB CANDLE BURNING MAGICK

You Will Need:

*Goddess Candle

*God Candle

*Incense

*Green Candle

*Good Luck Oil

*Black Candle

*Banishing Oil

*Petitioner Candle

Build your altar. Place the Petitioner candle beneath the Goddess candle and place the green and black candles beneath the God candle. Light the incense. Anoint the black candle with banishing oil and say,

"Empower this candle to absorb all negative forces acting upon me. As this candle burns, let it powers engulf all obstacles in my way, leaving my path clear for success."

Light the black candle. Anoint green candle with good luck oil and say,

"I empower this candle to bring me good luck, prosperity and success in acquiring a new and better job. As this candle burns, so might it be a beacon for good fortune and prosperity." Light the green candle.

You need not anoint the petitioner candle, but focus strongly on this person (if it is yourself, see yourself in your new job) as you light it, saying,

"As this candle represents {name}, let it be a beacon for positive forces and energies. As this candle burns bright, so does the light of {names}'s heart burn bright with ambition and desire for a new, better job."

Concentrate firmly, directing your power to the petitioner candle, which is receiving the energy from the green candle that is burning. After ten minutes or so of concentration, extinguish the candles in the reverse order in which you lit them. Each day, repeat the spell, moving the green candle two inches closer to the petitioner. Your spell is complete when the two candles touch.

A petitioner candle is a candle for the person the spell is being done for (so a colour that represents them.
The God and Goddess candle can be a candle shaped to represent them.

BLESSING A NEW HOME, HOME CLEANSING

Home-cleansing methods are of great importance in African-American hoodoo folk-magic. Here is a simple procedure for blessing a new home and ridding a house of any unwanted spiritual influences.

Wash down the woodwork and floors with Chinese Wash (or Van Van Oil in water) from back to front and out the front door and throw the remaining wash water out the front door or in the front yard. If there is no front yard, carry some of the wash water to the nearest street intersection or crossroads and throw it to the East.

Then use a brand new broom to sweep the house from back to front and out the front door. Some folks also like to sprinkle Van Van Powder at the front threshold and sweep that away from the house. After cleaning as above, put down pinches of salt in the corners of each room or, if you are in a hurry, four pinches of salt at the four outside corners of the house. If you cannot get Van Van Oil, Black Pepper Oil will work just fine.

BASIC LOCATION SPELL

This is a basic spell to locate anyone no matter where they're at.

You will need:

* 4 blue candles

* a goblet filled 3/4 of the way with water

* jasmine incense

* a quiet, undisturbed place

Put the 4 candles around you- one north, one south, one east, one west. Light the candles and the incense. Sit in the centre of the candles, facing west. Put the goblet in front of you. Invoke the element of water. Repeat 4 times: "Let the water show the location of (person's name)."

TO RECEIVE A CALL

All required is a piece of paper, pen/pencil, and a straight pin. Write the person's name twice on the paper, making a circle by connecting the beginnings and ends of the names together. Mentally connect with the person, asking that they please call you, and pierce the paper in the middle of the circle. Place the charm by the phone. This spell works in ways of 5, from what I was told, along the path of 5 minutes, 5 hours, 5 days.

CAST A WITCH'S LUCKY CANDLE SPELL

Take an orange candle anointed with cinnamon oil, clove, or lotus oil. Light the candle and say 3 times:

"Brimstone, the moon, and witches fire,

Candlelight's bright spell,

Good luck shall I now acquire,

Work thy magic well.

Midnight twelve, the witching hour,

Bring the luck I seek.

By wax and wick now work thy power

As these words, I speak.

Harming none, this spell is done.

By the law of three, so mote it be!"

Do this spell at midnight.

DEBT BANISHING SPELL

Supplies:

*Rolled parchment, 2 inches wide and as long as you like

*One black pen

*One purple candle Oil of your choice

*Incense of your choice

Cleanse and consecrate all supplies with the four elements (earth, air, fire, and water).

List all your debts on the parchment. Draw a banishing pentacle on the back of the parchment. Carve a banishing pentacle on the candle. Place the rolled parchment in the candle holder then tighten the candle on top. Think of banishing your debts. Think of the feeling of happiness and relief when the debts are banished.

Light the candle. Take the candle to the East quarter and ask that the Sylphs send your message of debt-banishment out to the universe in a safe and protective way, and ask that prosperity return to you in the same manner. Put the candle back on the altar and, in your own words, ask Juno to banish the debt and replace with prosperous energy. Allow the candle to burn completely. The paper will catch fire, so watch what type of holder you are using (glass will break) and that the candle holder is on a fire-safe surface.

As the candle burns, concentrate on banishing your debts, your feelings of relief and happiness, and the coming prosperity.

BATH SPELL FOR NEGATIVITY

Place 1/2 cup vinegar, a bunch of fresh rue and 1 tablespoon of salt in your bath. Light a white and a blue candle. Imagine yourself surrounded by blue light, giving you positive energy. Visualize all of the negative energy leaving your body through every pore.

TO CLEANSE MAGICKAL SPACE

Chant:

"Incense, air of high refine

Purify this space of mine.

Purged and purified be this place

That I have chosen as magickal space.

Herbs of Mother Earth give blessings here to me

This rite, this sacred sphere.

Protect and cleanse this sacred place

Hollow it now as my magickal space."

Walk around the space you're cleansing with the lit incense chanting this, hands up to the moon/sun/sky moving clockwise in a circle. Do this at least 3 times or until you feel all energy is positive.

HERBAL REMEDIES

CHAMOMILE

This popular beverage herb can calm jangled nerves, relieve stomach distress, prevent ulcers, speed their healing, and help fight infection. How to: For tea, 2 to 3 heaping teaspoons per cup, steeped 10 to 20 minutes. Up to 3 cups per day.

CHINESE EPHEDRA

Commonly used to treat colds and asthma, Chinese ephedra (Ma Huang) can also raise blood pressure and cause insomnia and other problems. warning: Prior to using Chinese ephedra, seek advice from a healthcare practitioner, especially if you are pregnant or nursing. It should not be given to children under 13.

COMFREY

This plant contains allantoin, which promotes the growth of new cells and gives it value as a wound treatment. how to: Place a bruised leaf on clean cuts or scrapes. Cover with a bandage. Warning: Do not use internally.

DANDELION

Despised as a weed, dandelion can help relieve premenstrual bloating. Preliminary studies suggest possible anti-inflammatory effects. How to: For tea, 1/2 ounce dried leaf per cup, steeped 10 minutes. Up to 3 cups per day.

FEVERFEW

Several studies confirm feverfew's value in preventing migraines. how to: Chew two leaves a day, or take a pill or capsule containing 85milligrams of leaf material (feverfew is quite bitter). For tea, 1/2 to 1 teaspoon per cup, steeped 5 to 10 minutes. Up to 2 cups per day.

GARLIC

When chewed or chopped, garlic is a potent natural antibiotic; it also has anti-viral properties. It reduces cholesterol and helps prevent the formation of internal blood clots that trigger heart attacks. How to: In food, season to taste. For tea, steep 6 cloves in a cup of cool water for 6 hours.

GINGER

Ginger prevents motion sickness and may help prevent the internal blood clots that trigger heart attacks. How to: For motion sickness, take 2 to 3 capsules of 500 milligrams 30 minutes before departure. For tea, 2 teaspoons powdered or grated root per cup, steeped 10 minutes. Up to 3 cups per day.

GINSENG

Ginseng stimulates the immune system, helps protect the liver from toxins and increases stamina. In one animal experiment, it also increased sexual activity. How to: Follow package directions for teas, capsules, tablets, and tinctures.

GOLDENSEAL

Studies show that this herb has antibiotic action. How to: For tea, 1/2 to 1 teaspoon powdered root per cup, steeped 10 minutes. Up to 2 cups per day.

LICORICE

Licorice can soothe sore throats and treat ulcers. How to: For a sore throat, add a pinch of root to tea. For ulcers, 1/2 teaspoon of powder per cup, boiled 10 minutes. Up to 2 cups per day. warning: Large doses can be dangerous.

RASBERRY LEAF

This premier pregnancy herb is widely used to treat morning sickness and uterine irritability, and to help prevent threatened miscarriage. How to: For tea, 1 to 2 teaspoons per cup, steeped 10 minutes. Up to 3 cups per day.

ROSEHIPS

The "hip" is the part that remains when the petals fall off the flower. Rose hips contain vitamin C. How to: For tea, 2 to 3 teaspoons per cup, steeped 10 minutes. Drink as needed.

SENNA

This herb is a powerful laxative. Senna tastes terrible, so most herbalists recommend a tincture or a commercial product. To avoid abdominal distress, do not take more than the package directions specify.

SLIPPERY ELM BARK

Historically used to soothe sore throats, coughs, and upset stomachs, this beneficial bark is still available in bulk and in herbal cough drops and throat lozenges. How to: For tea, 1 to 3 teaspoons of powdered bark per cup, boiled and simmered 15 minutes. Up to 3 cups per day.

SPEARMINT/PEPPERMINT

For indigestion, try a cup of mint tea after eating. How to: For tea, 1 teaspoon fresh or 2 teaspoons dried per cup, steeped 10 minutes. Reheat if desired. Up to 3 cups per day. For a relaxing bath, fill a cloth bag with a few handfuls of dried or fresh leaves, and run water over it.

UVA URSI

Research has shown that this bitter herb has diuretic and urinary antiseptic effects. Use it in addition to mainstream medical treatment. How to
One teaspoon per cup boiled 10 minutes. Up to 3 cups per day.

HERBOLOGY DEFINITIONS

Alterative - Producing a healthful change without perception

Anodyne - Relieves pain

Anthelmintic - A medicine that expels worms

Aperient - Gently laxative without purging

Aromatic - A stimulant, spicy

Astringent - Causes contraction and arrests discharges

Antibilious - Acts on the bile, relieving biliousness

Antiemetic - Stops vomiting

Antileptic - Relieves seizures

Antiperiodic - Arrests morbid periodic movements

Anthilic - Prevents formation of stones in urinary organs

Antirheumatic - Relieves rheumatism

Antiscorbutic - Cures or prevents scurvy

Antiseptic - aims at stopping putrification

Antispasmodic - Relieves or prevents spasms

Antisyphilitic- Having affect or curing STD

Carminative - Expels gas in the bowels

Carthatic - Evacuating from the bowels

Cephalic - Remedies used in diseases of the head

Cholagogue - Increases flow of bile

Condiment - Improves flavor of food

Demulcent - Soothing, relieves inflammation

Deobstruent - Removes obstruction

Depurative - Purifies the blood

Detergent - Cleansing to boils, ulcers, wounds etc

Diaphoretic - Produces perspiration

Discutient - Dissolves and heals tumors

Diuretic - Increases flow of urine

Emetic - Produces vomiting

Emmenagogue - Promotes menstruation

Emollient - Softens and soothes inflammation

Esculent - Eatable as food

Expectorant - Facilitates expectoration

Febrifuge - Abates and reduces fever

Hepatic - For diseases of the liver

Hepatic - Remedy for skin diseases of all types

Laxative - Promotes bowel action

Lithontriptic - Dissolves calculi in urinary organs

Maturating - Ripens or brings boils to a head

Mucilaginous - Soothing to all inflammations

Nauseant - Produces vomiting

Nervine - Acts specifically on nervous system, stops nervous excitement

Ophthalmic - For eye diseases

Parturient - Induces and promotes labor at childbirth

Pectoral - For chest infections

Refrigerant - Cooling

Resolvent - Dissolves boils and tumors

Rubefacient - Increases circulation and produces red skin

Sedative - Nerve tonic, promotes sleep

Sialogogue - Increases secretion of saliva

Stomachic - Strengthen stomach, relieves indigestion

Styptic - Stops bleeding

Sudorfic - Produces profuse perspiration

Tonic - Remedy which is invigorating and strengthing

Vermifuge - Expels worms from the system

WITCHES LADDER FOR COMFORT AND BLESSING

Take a long blue cord or ribbon, and collect 7 symbols to hang from it -- things like gray feathers for protection during sleep, sprigs of healing herbs, garlic for healing and protection, small talismans, conjure bags, charms - you get the idea. The important thing is that the symbols should represent comfort, protection, and healing. Tie them to the cord and charge it with comforting power.

CRYSTALS AND GEMSTONES FOR HEALING

AGATE

Good for transmutation; helps with the emotion of acceptance; gives a mellow, blended aspect; beneficial in stomach area.

AGATE/BOTSWANA

Use with high-pressure oxygen therapy; smoke inhalation.

AGATE/FIRE

Master healer with color therapy; enhances all essences; grounds and balances; sexual & heart chakra binder; burns energy.

AGATE/MOSS

Emotional priorities; mental priorities; colon, circulatory, pancreas & pulses; blood sugar balance; agriculture.

AGATE/PICTURE

L & R brain imbalances; i.e. epilepsy, autism, dyslexia; visual problems; blood circulation to the brain; apathy is eased.

ALEXANDRITE

Low self-esteem & difficulty centering imply need; central nervous system disorders; spleen & pancreas.

AMBER

Memory loss; eccentric behavior; anxiety; inability to make decisions; thyroid, inner ear & neural-tissue strengthener; activates altruistic nature; realization of the spiritual intellect.

AMETHYST

Headaches; blood sugar imbalance; L-brain imbalances; edginess; facilitates healing; inner peace; psychic insight; stimulates third eye; aid for meditation, spiritual opening & internal surrender.

ANHYDRITE

Heavy metal maism is alleviated.

AQUAMARINE

Fluid retention; coughs; fear; thymus gland; calms nerves; problems with eyes, ears, jaw, neck, stomach, teeth; Mental clarity; meditation.

ATACAMITE

Genitals; VD; thyroid; parasympathetic ganglia.

AVENTURINE

Eliminates psychosomatic ills; fear; skin diseases; nearsightedness; positive attitude; creative insight.

AZURITE

Arthritis & joints; surfaces psychic blocks that form physical blocks; helps one let go of old belief systems; dissolves fear & helps transform it into understanding.

AZURITE-MALACHITE

Skin diseases; anorexia; calms anxiety; lack of discipline; powerful healing force to the physical body; emotional release.

BERYL

Laziness; hiccoughs; swollen glands; eye diseases; bowel cancer.

BLOODSTONE/HELIOTROPE

Circulation; all purpose healer & cleanser; stomach & bowel pain; purifies bloodstream; bladder; strengthens blood purifying organs.

CARNELIAN

Grounding; stimulates curiosity & initiative; focuses attention on the present moment; use with citrine on lower 3 chakras; digestion.

CHALCEDONY

Touchiness; melancholy; fever; gallstones; leukemia; eye problems; stimulates maternal feelings & creativity. release.

CHRYSOCOLLA

Emotional balance & comforter; alleviates fear, guilt & nervous tension; facilitates clairvoyance; arthritis; feminine disorders; eases labor & birth; thought amplifier.

CHRYSOLITE

Inspiration; prophecy; toxemia; viruses; appendicitis.

CHRYSOPRASE

Gout; eye problems; alleviates greed, hysteria & selfishness; VD; depression; promotes sexual organ strength.

CITRINE QUARTZ

Heart, kidney, liver & muscle healer; appendicitis; gangrene; red & white corpuscles; digestive tract; cleanses vibrations in the atmosphere; creativity; helps personal clarity; will bring out problems in the solar plexus & the heart; eliminates self-destructive tendencies.

CLEAR QUARTZ

Transmitter & amplifier of healing energy & clarity; balancer, channeler of universal energy & unconditional love; all purpose healer; programmable.

DIAMOND

All brain diseases; pituitary & pineal glands; draws out toxicity, poison remedy.

DIOPSITE & ENSTATITE

Organ rejection; heart, lung & kidney stimulation; self-esteem.

EILAT STONE

Tissue & skeletal regeneration; detoxification; antidepressant; karmic life acceptance.

EMERALD

Radiation toxicity; all mental illness; circulatory & neurological disorders; transmits balance, healing & patience; increases psychic & clairvoyant abilities; meditation; keener insight into dreams.

FLOURITE

Bone disorders; anesthetic; hyperkinesis; ability to concentrate; balances polarities; 3rd eye center; mental capacity & intellect.

GARNET/RHODOLITE

Capillaries; skin elasticity; protection from pre- cancerous conditions.

GARNET/SPESSARTINE

Bad dreams; depression; anger; self-esteem; hemorrhages; hormone imbalances; inflammations; sexual disease.

HEMATITE

Blood cleanser & purifier; self-esteem; augments meridian flows; aids in astral projection.

HERKIMER DIAMOND

Enhances dream state; helps alleviate stress; draws toxicity from physical form; balances polarities; increases healing ability; develops ability to "give".

JADE

Kidney, heart, larynx, liver, parathyroid, spleen, thymus, thyroid & parasympathetic ganglia healer; strengthens body; longevity.

JASPER/GREEN

Constipation; ulcers; intestinal spasms; bladder, gallbladder & general healer; clairvoyance; balances healer's auric field.

JASPER/PICTURE

Skin, kidneys, thymus & their neurological tissues; betters the immune system; past life recall; overactivity in dream state & hallucinations show a need for it.

JASPER/RED

Liver; stomach troubles & infections.

JASPER/YELLOW

Endocrine system tissue; thymus; pancreas; sympathetic ganglia stimulation; etheric body alignment.

JET

Feminine disorders; teeth; stomach pain; glandular swelling; fevers; hair loss; alignment of the lower spine.

KUNZITE

Alcoholism; anorexia; arthritis; epilepsy; gout; headaches; colitis; retardation; memory loss; schizophrenia & manic-depression; phobias; emotional equilibrium; thyroid malignancy; gums; pain; self-esteem.

LAPIS

Neuralgia; melancholy; fevers; inflammations; penetrates subconscious blockages; throat chakra; a sore throat; energy focuser for teachers, lecturers & speakers, mental & spiritual cleanser; used on 3rd eye for meditation;eliminates old & negative emotions; use with other healing stones; thought form amplification; helps in creating mantras.

LAZULITE

Frontal lobe stimulation; hypertension; liver diseases; immune system.

MALACHITE

Draws out impurities on all levels; balances L & R brain functions; mental illness; co-ordination and vision; radiation eliminator; evil eye protector; all purpose healer, especially in solar plexus & good for healers.

MOONSTONE

Soothes & balances the emotions; helps eliminate the fear of "feeling"; encourages inner growth & strength; aids peace & harmony & psychic abilities; aligns vertebrae; digestive aid.

MORGANITE

Larynx; lungs; thyroid; parasympathetic nervous system; major muscle tissues.

NATROLITE

Color; lower intestines; thyroid; sciatic nerve; parasympathetic nervous system.

OBSIDIAN

Protects the gentle from being abused; stabilizer; stomach, intestine &I general muscle tissue healer; bacterial & viral inflammations.

ONYX

Objective thinking; spiritual inspiration; control of emotions & passions, help eliminate negative thinking, apathy, stress & neurological disorders; also used as a heart, kidney, nerve, skin, capillary, hair, eye and nail strengthener.

OPAL/CHERRY

Red corpuscle & blood disorders; depression; apathy; lethargy; intuition & joy.

OPAL/DARK

Reproductive organs; spleen & pancreas; filters red corpuscles & aids white corpuscles; bone marrow; depression, esp. of sexual origin; balances; amplifies creative & intuitive thought; grounds radical emotional body.

OPAL/JELLY

Spleen & abdominal diseases; cellular reproductive problems; helps absorb nutrients; minimizes wide mood swings; mystical thought amplifier.

OPAL/LIGHT

Balances L & R brain hemispheres for neural disorders; stimulates white corpuscles; helps bring the emotions to mystical experiences; aids abdomen, pituitary & thymus problems.

PEARL

Eliminates emotional imbalances; helps one master the heart chakra; aids stomach, spleen, intestinal tract & ulcer problems.

PERIDOT

Protects against nervousness; helps alleviate spiritual fear; aids in healing hurt feelings & bruised egos; incurs strength & physical vitality; aligns subtle bodies; amplifies other vibrational energies & positive emotional outlook; helps liver & adrenal function.

PYRITE

Help purify the bloodstream and upper respiratory tract; upper intestines; digestive aid; nervous exhaustion; grounding.

QUARTZ/SOLUTION

Lymphatic cancer & circulatory problems; helps the psychologically inflexible.

RHODOCHROSITE

Narcolepsy & narcophobia; poor eyesight; extreme emotional trauma; mental breakdown; nightmares & hallucinations; astral body; kidneys; clears solar plexus of blocked energy; unconditional love & forgiveness; evil eye protection; helps one utilize the creative power of the higher energy centers.

RHODONITE

Inner ear; alleviates anxiety; confusion & mental unrest; promotes calm, self-worth, confidence & enhanced sensitivity.

RHYOLITE

Balances emotions; self-worth; enhances capacity to love; aligns emotional & spiritual bodies; stimulates clarity of self-statement.

ROSE QUARTZ

Heart chakra opener; love & self-acceptance healer for emotional wounds; dissipates anger & tension.

ROYAL AZEL (SUGALITE or LUVALITE)

L & R hemisphere balance; opens crown chakra; heart statement; increases altruism, visions & general understanding; protects against negative vibrations; helps one gain power to balance the physical body.

RUBY

Heart chakra; balances love & all spiritual endeavors; self-esteem; strengthens neurological tissues around the heart; prevents miscarriages.

RUTILE

Alleviates blockages within the psyche from childhood pressures.

SAPPHIRE

Spiritual enlightenment; inner peace; colic; rheumatism; mental illness; pituitary; the metabolic rate of glandular functions; anti-depressant; aids psychokinesis, telepathy, clairvoyance & astral projection; personal statement; also for pain.

SARDONYX

Mental self-control; depression; anxiety & especially for grief.

SMITHSONITE

Eases fear of interpersonal relationships; merges astral & emotional bodies; balances perspective.

SMOKY QUARTZ

Stimulates Kundalini energy; cleanses & protects the astral field; draws out distortion on all levels; good for hyperactivity & excess energy; grounding.

SODALITE

Oversensitivity; helps intellectual understanding of a situation; awakens 3rd eye; cleanses the mind.

SPINEL

Leg conditions, when worn on solar plexus; powerful general healer; detoxification aid.

TIGER'S EYE

Mind focused; helps purify the blood system of pollution & toxins; psychic vision; grounding.

TOPAZ

Balances emotions; calms passions; gout; blood disorders; hemorrhages; increases poor appetite; general tissue regeneration; VD; tuberculosis; reverses aging; spiritual rejuvenation; endocrine system stimulation; releases tension; feelings of joy.

TOURMALINE

Dispels fear & negativity & grief; calms nerves; concentration & eloquence improve; genetic disorders, cancer & hormones regulated; raises vibrations; charisma; universal law; tranquil sleep.

TOURMALINE/BLACK

Arthritis; dyslexia; syphilis; heart diseases; anxiety; disorientation; raises altruism; deflects negativity; neutralizes distorted energies, i.e. resentment & insecurity.

TOURMALINE/RUBELLITE

Creativity; fertility; balances passive or aggressive nature.

TOURMALINE/GREEN

Creativity; opens heart chakra; immune system; psychological problems with the father; blood pressure; asthma; balancer; eliminates conflict within.

TOURMELINNE/BLUE (INDICOLITE)

Lungs, larynx; thyroid; parasympathetic nerves.

TOURMALINE/WATERMELON

Heart chakra healer; imparts a sense of humour to those who need it; balancer; eliminates guilt; nervous system; integration, security & self-containment.

TURQUOISE

Master healer; protects against environmental pollutants; strengthens anatomy & guards against all disease; improved absorption of nutrients; tissue regeneration; subtle body alignment & strengthening; eye disorders.

WISHING POWDER

You Will Need:

* The Great Outdoors (This could be your backyard, a park, or forest -- any place where the wishing powder will land on the earth when you release it).

* Anything else you feel you need to personalize your wish.

You will need to craft the wishing powder ahead of time. You can either do this at home in a Circle or, if you don't mind taking your mortal and pestle along with you, you can make it outside where you plan to use it. (This isn't too hard to do if you're staying in your own backyard).

* 2 parts sage

* 1 part sandalwood

* 1 part Tonka beans(look on amazon)

Grind, mix, and empower.

If you're feeling adventurous, customize your wishing powder to the wish you'll be making. (Example: Crushed rose petals for bringing love into your life). Find a spot to make our wishes from.

Take a handful of the wishing powder and begin concentrating on your wishes. (Please do not put yourself in danger to make a wish. A wish is just as powerful whether it's made standing on a rock on the side of a steep hill or standing in a field). Put your energy and wish into the powder you are holding. When it feels like you can no longer hold the energy, let it fly. As the powder settles to the ground, visualize your wishes joining with the Earth, gaining power and strength.

As always, remember the Rule of Three when making your wish. After putting the energy out there, it's impossible to call it back. Remember the old saying, "Be careful what you wish for, you may get it." If you are worried about where to get Tonka Beans (as needed for the above wishing spell), you can do an easy search for them through any search engine to find them. Vanilla Beans/pods are a Substitute

HEMATITE GROUNDING

Hematite is the all-purpose grounding (energy-balancing) stone, not to mention a beautiful ornament. Tell, or charge all your troubles to or into the rock, then put it on the ground overnight, so that the negative energy will soak into the Earth and become neutral.

MOJO BAG SPELLS.

1. To Bring Justice
2. The Bag of Retribution
3. For Safe Travel
4. To Increase Male Fertility
5. For Safe Childbirth
6. The Bag of Riches
7. The Lovers Bag
8. To Uncover the Truth
9. Personal Power Mojo Bag
10. For Protection

1. To Bring Justice

The energy of this bag will work well when you find yourself caught in a situation where you are the victim of an injustice.

But a word of caution, make sure you are the innocent party here before you decide to use this spell. Karma, the powers that be, whatever you want to call the incredible energy that makes this magic work, is not selective. You should be absolutely one hundred percent sure that you are the innocent victim in this situation and that you have not contributed to the negative circumstances in any way.

Because justice will—most definitely—be meted out.

This is also the bag you want to create if you are involved with litigation and the judicial system.

Correspondences:

Moon Phase: waxing to full moon
Day: Thursday
Planet: Jupiter
Colors: blue, indigo, purple
Herbs: cinnamon, nutmeg, sage, marigold, hickory
Stones: tiger eye
Tarot Card: Justice

Fill this bag with the tarot card, the stone, and at least three of the herbs. If you're involved in a legal case, you might want to add a photo of the presiding judge or his signature, if it's available to you.

If you're the victim of an injustice, add personal effects belonging to the person who wronged you. Personal effects would include hair, fingernail clippings, a scrap of material from clothing, etc. If these items are not available to you, a photo or signature will do, or write his/her name on a piece of paper and add it to the ingredients.

Keep this bag hidden away in a secret spot for as long as the matter continues on in the court system, or until justice is reached. When it is over, dismantle the bag and dispose of the items off your property, burying them along a secluded lane or gravel road.

2. The Bag of Retribution

I make no bones about the fact that both light and shadow exists in magic, that the world is not divided into even and neatly ordered black and white regions, and that sometimes we will be required to step into a gray area. Whether for protection, retribution, or any number of very personal reasons, there may come a time when you will have to step into the shadows and grab its energy for your own use.
Don't fear the shadows. Often we have a clearer view once we've stepped out of the blinding light.

This bag will dole out retribution against someone who is deliberately wreaking havoc in people's lives; someone whose bad behavior, deviousness, abuse, and lack of conscience are putting innocent people at risk.

Correspondences

Moon Phase: waxing to dark moon
Day: Saturday
Colors: black, dark gray, indigo
Herbs: black poppy seeds, blackthorn, rue, willow, black pepper, cayenne pepper, *nightshade (*poisonous)
Stones: black onyx

Tarot Card: The Tower

Fill this bag with the tarot card, the stone, and at least three of the herbs. To these ingredients, you could add goofer dust, a small piece of paper on which you vent your feelings towards this person, and a photo or a name paper of the target. (A 'name paper' is simply a piece of paper upon which you've written the person's name.)

To keep this person bound from harming anyone else, until retribution has been doled out or karma exacted, keep this bag—and keep it under very particular circumstances. Obtain a small hand mirror, large enough to lay the bag in the center and circle it with a line of salt and graveyard dirt. You are, in effect, trapping this person, keeping them under your control. Keep this spell in a *very* safe place, where the line of salt and graveyard dirt will not be disturbed or broken. I've done just such a spell, and I kept it hidden beneath my dresser with a silver bowl laid over the top so that my cats wouldn't climb beneath the dresser and disturb it.

Every dark moon carefully brings this spell out, strengthen it with more salt or graveyard dirt if you see any weak spots in the circle; vent your feelings in no uncertain terms at this bag, and thus this person; spit upon it if you are so inclined. Then carefully return it to its secret place, until the next dark moon.

Steel yourself. This is a very potent spell and the retribution which the universe *will* dole out can be very startling and often disturbing.

When all is said and done, dispose of the articles of this spell quickly and very much *off* your property.

3. For Safe Travel

You will find this mojo bag in my own vehicle, as well as in the vehicles of two of my children. This is the first thing I did when they very proudly purchased their first cars. I remember tucking it beneath the driver's seat of my son's van and was surprised to find it hanging boldly from his rearview mirror the next day. My daughter went through a baptism by fire when she experienced two accidents on a busy Omaha freeway, totaling both vehicles both times. She walked away from the incidents completely unscathed.

Correspondences:

Moon Phase: waxing to full moon, the full moon being most favorable
Day: Saturday
Planet: Saturn
Colors: black, dark gray, indigo
Herbs: plantain, calamus root
Stones: tiger eye
Tarot Card: The Chariot

Fill the bag with the tarot card, the stone, and *Both* herbs. This is very important. The combination of the plantain and the calamus root creates a very potent protective energy. I'm fortunate that plantain grows freely in my yard; I harvest and dry some every year for my own use.

To this bag, you may also want to add a dash of sea salt and perhaps even some personal effects belonging to the person/people who will be traveling in this vehicle on a regular basis. Keep this bag in the vehicle at all times. Every few months I take my bag out, at the time of the full moon, and re-consecrate it with the four elements.
This is a very easy, very simple thing to do:

1. Sprinkle the bag with salt, saying:
"I consecrate this bag with the power of Earth."
2. Hold the bag in the smoke of lit incense, allowing the smoke to envelop the bag, saying:
"I consecrate this bag with the power of Air."
3. Hold the bag in your left hand and a lit red candle in your right. Circle the bag clockwise with the candle, saying:
"I consecrate this bag with the power of Fire."
4. Dip your fingers into a small bowl of water, and flick the drops upon the bag, saying:
"I consecrate this bag with the power of Water...
This bag is now consecrated and divine, bound to aid me in my magical endeavors."

4. To Increase Male Fertility

While many of us have started families and had children without giving it a second thought, there are countless couples out there devastated by the fact that they cannot conceive. Often issues involved with fertility may be found with the woman, but sometimes this isn't so—sometimes it's the man who has issues with physical infertility.

This bag is for him.

Correspondences

Moon Phase: waxing to full moon, the full moon being the most favorable
Day: Sunday
Planet: Sun
Colors: gold, orange, white, yellow
Herbs: frankincense, poppy seeds, rice, sunflower
Stones: hematite (associated with the root chakra)

Tarot Card: The Emperor

Fill the bag with the tarot card, at least three of the herbs listed; and I strongly recommend that rice is one of those included.

The practice of magic can get pretty earthy. For anyone not up to my next suggestion, don't worry about the potency of the magic created by your will and intent, the magic will still work even if you don't want to add the following ingredient. However, for those of you who wish, to this bag add a small cloth with the man's semen upon it.

Keep this bag in your bedroom, the nearer your bed the better—lying on the floor beneath it, tucked into a shelf on the headboard, or kept beneath your pillow. You get the idea.

5. For Safe Childbirth

We're very fortunate to live in a country that provides excellent medical care for women during pregnancy and the experience of childbirth. However, once in a while, the unexpected can happen, and when it does, it's nice to feel the hand of Divinity close by—healing, protecting, and guiding. This is especially desirable when the Divinity is feminine.

This bag is *Not* to be relied on in lieu of the good solid care of an obstetrician. Instead, this bag is meant to be kept close to you through the wondrous nine-month journey you are on. And when the time comes, it's meant to be tucked into your overnight bag and taken with you when you go to experience the grand adventure of childbirth.

Correspondences

Moon Phase: waxing to full, the full moon being the most favorable
Day: Monday
Planet: the Moon (associated with the Mother Goddess)
Colors: silver, white, gray, blue
Herbs: moonwort, gardenia, jasmine, myrrh, lily
Stones: moonstone, chalcedony, crystal quartz
Tarot Card: The Empress

Fill this bag with the tarot card, the stone you've chosen, and at least three of the herbs.

To this bag, you may also want to add some of the following items: a lock of your hair, a photo of your own mother, perhaps an ultrasound photo of the baby, a Virgin Mary medal, a Goddess pendant, a small statuette of the Goddess, the Virgin, etc.

6. The Bag of Riches

This mojo bag deals with prosperity. This does not mean that you will become obscenely rich. It's not about that; it never is. The Bag of Riches is a little magical insurance to make sure that your purse never runs dry, to see that you always have enough money to put food on the table, clothes on your back, and a roof over your head. This mojo bag can also be used when a specific amount of money is needed for a particular reason.

Correspondences

Moon Phase: waxing to full moon, with the full moon being the most favorable
Day: Thursday
Planet: Jupiter
Colors: green

Herbs: mint, basil, black poppy seeds, dill, marjoram, patchouli
Stones: adventurine
Tarot Card: nine of pentacles

To this bag you could also add a dollar bill with your wishes and intentions written upon it, especially if you need a certain amount of money for something in particular; a series of coins—a quarter, nickel, dime, and penny; a special coin, if you have one, such as a gold dollar, etc. It is particularly advantageous to carry this bag in your purse or keep it near your wallet.

7. The Lover's Bag

Are you drawn to a special person and need a little magical push so that this individual will become aware of you? There is always controversy over love spells that are aimed at a particular person. Some consider this type of magic a binding; others consider it unethical on many levels in general. But I feel we should always give love a chance.

If you're meant to be together, the universe will shine upon you, and it will be so. If it's not meant to be a lasting relationship, perhaps there's a life lesson you will learn from this individual, and maybe that's why you were drawn to them in the first place.

If love is calling and your heart fluttering at the sight of someone special, but they don't seem to know that you exist, this is the mojo bag for you.

Correspondences

Moon Phase: waxing to full moon
Day: Friday
Planet: Venus

Colors: red
Herbs: rose petals, cardamom, ginger, coriander, hibiscus, red geranium
Stone: rose quartz
Tarot Card: The Lovers

To this bag, you will definitely want to add some personal effects. Your own items could include a lock of your hair; fingernail clippings; a Kleenex that you've blotted lipstick on, leaving an imprint of your lips; a photo; your signature; etc.

If it's at all possible, add similar personal effects belonging to the target. If you're not able to obtain any items of this nature, at least include a name paper. A love note, or love letter, written by you to the target, telling him/her all those things you'd like to say to them would be an excellent item to add to this bag. Be sure to add at least three of the herbs listed, and I strongly suggest that rose petals be one of them.

8. To Uncover the Truth

If you're involved in a situation and you suspect there is deception, it's time to discover the truth of the matter. This mojo bag will do just that, but don't expect grand Hollywood-type special effects. Real magic is so much more subtle; it does not break the laws of physics—usually; and sometimes the results will be completely unexpected and out of the blue—from a source you never would have guessed, at the time you least expect it, and with a revelation that will either cast a blazing light on the truth or quietly reveal imperative information.

That's the way this mojo bag will work.

Correspondences

Moon Phase: waxing to full moon, with the full moon being most favorable
Day: Wednesday
Planet: Mercury
Colors: yellow
Herbs: slippery elm, adder's tongue, cloves, drawing powder
Stones: agate
Tarot Card: The Moon

To this bag add at least two of the herbs listed, and it would bode you well to add a paper to this bag upon which you explain the situation and your desire to know the truth.

9. The Personal Power Mojo Bag

Personal Power Bag for Women:
For this mojo bag, we're going to draw on the energy of the High Priestess. Within her lays the power of the Feminine Divine. She will represent the inner core of all women, where magic resides, where the witch exists—"There's a little witch in every woman.", so goes the saying. All of these archetypes—the priestess, the goddess, the witch—represents and emphasizes personal power.

Correspondences

Moon Phase: full moon
Day: Monday
Planet: Moon
Colors: blue, silver, white
Herbs: moonwort, lotus, myrrh, gardenia, cardamom, belladonna, thyme, lilac, apple blossoms, violet, wormwood
Stones: moonstone, blue lace agate, clear quartz crystal
Tarot Card: The High Priestess

Personal Power Bag for Men:

For the man, we're going to draw on the energy of The Magician. Within him lays the power of the masculine, the Priest—the Elder, the Shaman, the Sorcerer, the Wizard. The Magician holds the mysticism of the four elements within his hands and the will needed to create magic. These archetypes represent personal power.

Correspondences

Moon Phase: full moon
Day: Sunday
Planet: Sun
Colors: yellow, orange, white
Herbs: carnation, juniper, rowan, sunflower, St. John's Wort, mistletoe
Stones: amber, carnelian, tiger's eye
Tarot Card: The Magician

To this bag, add at least three of the herbs and one of the stones listed. You could also add an image of the God/Goddess, such as a pendant or small statuary. I've seen some very tiny and beautiful ones in new-age shops. If you have a patron god/goddess, you could also add images, herbs, stones, objects, etc., that are special and unique to His/Her energy.

Add to this bag images or objects that represent power to you—an object from your workplace, if you feel this is where your power lays; a photo of your children; tokens of past success; slips of paper filled with personal affirmations; images of men or women who represent success and power to you, such as your mother/father, grandmother/grandfather, or a public figure.

10. For Protection

The nine of wands is a card which represents 'The Warrior', and it's the energy of this card we're going to call upon for this mojo bag. I have to say, along with this magic, you have to reclaim your personal power and find belief in yourself in order to conquer those people who might wish bad things upon you—either subconsciously through envy, jealousy, spite; or deliberately through the magic of hexes and curses; or through other mundane actions such as sabotage, gossip, deceit, etc.

The contents of this bag will shield you from the onslaught of negativity mentioned above. It will also throw back upon your adversaries the very negativity they aim at you, and it will seal it there, where it belongs.

Correspondences

Moon Phase: waning to dark moon, with the dark moon being most favorable
Day: Saturday
Planet: Saturn
Colors: black
Herbs: anise, calamus, fennel, frankincense, blackthorn, elder, rue
Stones: black onyx, garnet, obsidian.
Tarot Card: nine of wands

To this bag add at least three of the herbs and one of the stones listed. I would also advise you to add a pinch each of the following ingredients: goofer dust, graveyard dirt, banishing powder, and salt. If you are aware of particular people who are giving you grief, you could add a name paper for each person. But I warn you, be very cautious about singling out individuals; you must be one hundred percent sure that this action is warranted. It is sometimes best to let the universe dole out retribution and punishment. Karma does indeed have a way of coming back to mete out justice.

HEALTH AND HEALING SPELLS.
1. Basic Candle Spell and Correspondences

Day: Thursday
Hour: 1st/8th hour after sunrise; 3rd/10th hour after sunset
Planet: Jupiter
Moon Phase: waxing/full, to bring good health; waning/dark, to banish illness
Color: green
Herbs: health- rosemary, sage, St. John's Wort; healing- garlic, fennel, thyme
Oil: Health & Healing oil
Incense: lavender or sandalwood
Stone: green jasper, jade, moss agate, blue-lace agate
Number: 3
Letters: C, L, U
Symbols: rune 'sigil', for healing; rune 'uruz', for physical health; triple ring
Deities: Horus

When your sacred space is created and secure, your candle anointed and rolled in the appropriate herbs, write this spell upon a piece of parchment paper. Recite it three times, and burn it in the flame of your spell candle- scattering the ashes to the wind to dispose of it.

"I cast now a healing spell for (name),
That there shall be unto thee,
Blessings of good health and healing,
By the power of three times three,

So mote it be."

2. To Cure an Illness (knot magic)

Traditionally knot magic is done with a nine-foot long red cord or ribbon. But for this healing spell, we're going to use the healing energy of the colour green. Make sure that you mark nine points on your green cord or ribbon, where nine knots will be tied.

The idea behind knot magic is that we tie up our intentions, as well as the energy that can manifest those intentions, within the knot. For this spell, we're going to grab the energy to banish illness on the night of the dark moon, or within three nights afterward. We'll cast the spell, tie the knots, and lay this cord aside to let the magic ferment. As the energy of the moon grows and builds towards the full moon, so does the energy contained within the knots. On the night of the full moon, we will untie each knot, unleashing the magic and manifestation.

Items needed:
1. A nine-foot long green cord/ribbon
2. Three votive candles- two black, one green
3. White pillar altar candle
4. Health & Healing oil
5. A blue lace agate stone
6. A red flannel bag

Assuming your space is prepared, your circle cast and quarters called, you will carve the name of the target on the green candle and anoint it with the Health & Healing Oil. Line the three votive candles upon your altar, the green candle being in the center. Light all your altar candles and incense, and get yourself seated and comfortable to work on your knots.

As you tie the knots, keep an image of the target before you on your altar, preferably a photograph, or an image visualized in your mind, if you don't have a picture.

Tie each knot to the following chant, and as you work from knot to knot, keep the chant going continuously. Take your time. Eventually, the chant may run together in a whispered frenzy. It also may become very mesmerizing, and you may feel 'floaty' and spacey by the time you reach the end of the ribbon. This is good, it means that you've put yourself in an alpha state, where magic is possible.

The Chant:
"Illness leave, go away,
Good health I bid you come to stay."

When the knots are tied, the chanting stopped, and the candle has burned down; add the ribbon, the blue-lace agate, and the remains of the candle wax to the red flannel bag. You can keep this bag on your altar till the full moon, if possible, if not- make sure you put it in a safe place till the time is ripe.

On the night of a full moon, you will seat yourself within a cast circle, and by the light of a white altar candle, you will begin to slowly untie the knots, releasing the magic. As you do so, chant the chant:

"I open now the healing gates;
Good health upon the one who waits,
(name)."

All the remnants of this spell- the ribbon, bag, stone, candle wax, can be disposed of by either burying it in the earth or burning everything and scattering the ashes to the wind.

3. Healing Crystal

I love the energy of crystals and stones, and I work with them often. I surround myself, my home, and my very person with this special magic. One very positive thing you can do to generate a warm and healing atmosphere in your home is to choose a crystal that resonates with you, bless it for healing and peace, and place it in an auspicious location in your house or apartment.

First, you'll have to choose a crystal- and this can be a delightful adventure and project in itself. Browse shops, taking your time. Look at as many as you need to. Hold them, handle them, until a particular crystal seems to call to you. After finding this treasure and purchasing it, you will take it home and bless it: holding the crystal in your hands, you will imbue it with your energy and intentions, feeling it warm as the energy is absorbed. Take your time during this process and enjoy.

You can use an altar to bless this crystal, making the process as ritualistic and detailed as you wish, or you can simply continue with just you and the stone.

If you have a patron god or goddess, call upon their energy to bless this stone, along with the vibrational tone from your own environment and the energy of your body, coupled with the will of your intentions. State aloud and clearly exactly what type of energy you wish this crystal to emanate, focusing on this type of energy, visualizing it moving through your body, your arms, down to your hands and into the crystal itself.

This crystal will sit in a special place, where its energy can spread and radiate throughout your living quarters. Every once in a while, if you feel the need, you can recharge this crystal, or you can cleanse it by holding it beneath running water, leaving it briefly in a bowl of sea salt, letting it sit beneath the moonlight- or in the sunlight- depending upon which energy you wish to work with.

PROTECTION SPELLS.

1. Basic Candle Spell and Correspondences
Day: Saturday
Hour: 1st/8th hour after sunrise; 3rd/10th hour after sunset
Planet: Saturn
Moon Phase: waxing/to bring protection to you; waning/to banish whatever you need protection from
Color: black
Herbs: fennel, mint, sage, thistle, night-shade (poisonous)- Nightshade is poisonous and can be absorbed through the skin. Handle it with gloved hands only- if you handle it at all! If you burn it, which I wouldn't advise, don't inhale the fumes.-, black pepper, cayenne pepper, garlic, dill- especially protects children
Oil: Banishing Oil or Mars Astrological Oil (good stuff)
Incense: sandalwood
Stone: obsidian, red jasper
Number: 8
Letters: H, Q, Z
Symbols: Earth symbol- write the name of who or what you want to be protected within it
Deities: Brigit (when seeking protection for children)

Using the correspondences above, set up your sacred space, dress your candle with oil and the herbs. What exactly is it that you feel you need protection from? If it's an individual and you are fortunate enough to have their photo in your possession, place it on a small mirror and circle it with salt and graveyard dirt, trapping them within. Burn the spell candle near this image. If it's a situation, create a mojo bag using these correspondences and the remains of your spell candle, inserting into the bag those items connected in some way with the troublesome situation or people involved.

2. A Vehicle Blessing

We use to make quite a few road trips with the family when the children were small, and before each new adventure, I would bless our vehicle to keep the occupants safe from an accident. I still do this periodically, not only to my own vehicle but with my children's vehicles, when I can get my hands on them.

The following blessing can be performed in conjunction with creating a mojo bag to hang in your vehicle or to conceal beneath the seat, its purpose being to keep you safe and prevent accidents. I included a spell for this bag in my first book: "Tarot: A Witch's Journey". You can perform this little ritual in the privacy of your enclosed garage, which I've done several times; or you can brave the neighbors' curiosity by performing this ritual in your driveway, which I've also done several times.

The Correspondences:

Note: You should know that I've had to modify the timing for this ritual on several occasions, in accordance with our travel plans, and that will work just fine. Also, if you have herbs that you personally work with for protection spells and that work for you, feel free to substitute them for this ritual. Below are the correspondences I use from my own Book of Shadows.

Day: Tuesday
Hour: 1st/8th hour after sunrise; 3rd/10th hour after sunset
Planet: Mars
Moon Phase: preferably waxing to full
Color: black or orange

Herbs: dill, fennel, rosemary, plantain...(use dill especially for the protection of children)
Oil: Mars Astrological Oil or a good protection oil of your choosing
Incense: sandalwood
Stone: black obsidian, red jasper, citrine, tiger eye
Symbol: the planetary symbol for Mars, and the symbol for Earth, as well as the invoking pentagram for Earth

Items needed:
1. Six candles: green (earth), yellow (air), red (fire), blue (water), white (spirit), black– for the cauldron
2. Your oil and incense
3. Small bowl of water & salt
4. Parchment paper on which you've written the spell you'll find below
5. Any of the herbs that you care to use in a mojo bag, to use in the ritual, or to place within the vehicle

Arrange the elemental candles around the vehicle in the pattern of a pentagram. If you're pinched for space, you can even arrange them upon the hood of the vehicle. Light the candles and the incense. Have the black spell candle dressed in oil and herbs and placed within your cauldron or a fire-proof receptacle. Light it as well. Using your oil, go around the vehicle and anoint the front, the back, the tires, and each of the doors with the oil, using the invoking pentagram for the earth.

I open the door and, with my bowl of salted water in hand, I asperge the interior of the vehicle. I've also been known to throw a dash of sea salt here and there, as well as some crushed sage.

Go then to the front of the vehicle, before the white candle of spirit and your cauldron containing the burning black spell candle.

Recite the spell below out loud, following the directions as you do so, and then burn the written spell in the flame of your spell candle, allowing the ashes to mingle with the melted wax. This can all be used later by adding it to your mojo bag.

The spell:
"I cast now a spell to protect
All those who will occupy this space,
Creating for them a sacred place."

"I bless this vehicle by the powers of the earth."(walk in a complete circle around your vehicle, carrying a bowl of salt, stopping before your cauldron candle)

"I bless this vehicle by the powers of the air."
(walk in a complete circle around your vehicle, carrying the burning incense, stopping before your cauldron candle)

"I bless this vehicle by the powers of fire."
(walk in a complete circle around your vehicle, carrying the burning white candle of spirit, stopping before your cauldron candle)

"I bless this vehicle by the powers of water."
(walk in a complete circle around your vehicle, carrying the bowl of water, stopping before your cauldron candle)

"As these elements protect and guard my magic circle,
So shall they protect and guard all those who ride in this vehicle.
I empower this spell three times three,
As I do will, so mote it be."

Gently lower the written spell to the flame of the black candle, igniting the parchment, and drop it into the cauldron to finish burning. Extinguish the elemental candles, but allow the black spell candle to burn itself out. Dismantle your circle, if you have cast one, and eat something to ground yourself. I've found that this spell can be quite draining for some reason, so don't neglect the last suggestion, and don't be surprised if you are very hungry at the end of it.

3. To Spite Your Face

One of the most frustrating foes to deal with is a person who is jealous and spiteful. This spell will deal with their energy, while most importantly, it will protect you from the fallout of their actions and their spitefulness.

Items needed:
1. A cauldron containing a nice little pile of burning herbs (slippery elm and sage would be nice, but sage will do), creating a respectable sized flame- you might want to use a small charcoal tablet, just to keep things going
2. A black votive candle
3. A photo of the target- if this is not available, their signature or a name paper will have to do
4. A red flannel bag
5. Three blossoms from a thorny plant, preferably a thistle; or three thorns- which are just as effective

Carve the target's name on the black spell candle, and sit it on your altar, near your cauldron. Light it- with glee and delight, knowing that you are lighting a flame beneath your enemies feet.

You will take their photo and, with the focused emotions you feel at this person and their actions, you will mark it, slash it, spit on it, stomp on it- or do something else even more dastardly to it, all the while maintaining the focus and intent of your actions. It's imperative that you do not loose sight of your intentions.

Burn this image in your cauldron, amidst the herbs and flames. When the fire has burned down, the black candle has burned itself out, and everything has cooled down– except your emotions and will– deposit the ashes and remnants of this spell into the red flannel bag.

Then add three blossoms or three thorns to the bag, one at a time.

With the first blossom/thorn, say:

"The first I add to freeze your speech."

With the second blossom/thorn, say:

"The second I add to halt your reach."

With the third blossom/thorn, say:

"The third I add to spite your face,
That you may wallow in disgrace."

Keep this bag in a safe and secret place, allowing the magic time to mature and ripen, that the target will feel the full effects.

4. The In-Law Spell

I have experienced within my lifetime the effects of one of the relationships that can be the most poisonous and destructive- in-laws. These people don't have to have a reason for disliking you; your existence is usually good enough reason. If you've reached what you feel is 'the end of no return' and contact with these people is proving destructive to your family and overly stressful, or even harmful to your health, it's time to bid them farewell. No, we're not going to harm them, nor banish them, we're just going to mark our territory and let the power of magic make it off limits to them.

Think of a tomcat and how he marks his territory. Basically, we're going to do the same thing, but without the urine. Instead, we're going to use the magic of the green witch to mark our space with the herb: oregano.

You're going to want a good-sized hefty cast-iron cauldron, some charcoal tablets to keep things going, and a plentiful quantity of oregano. You are going to get a good handful of oregano burning in your cauldron, and then tone it down so that it's smoldering and smoking up a storm. And no, you' probably won't like the smell of it- but it works like a charm- pun intended! The essence of the oregano will magically keep your in-laws at bay.

Carry this cauldron throughout your home, smudging every room, and most importantly- every entrance! And I do mean every entrance: garage doors, back doors, old cellar doors you haven't used in ages, portals, doggy doors, and windows- any opening into your home- smudge it!

You should also smudge a photograph of these in-laws. To add fuel to my fire, so to speak, I actually burned a photograph of them in my cauldron so that it was smoldering away with the oregano.

It's been years since I performed this unique and useful little spell...and it's been years since my threshold has seen the shadow of an in-law.

1. Shed Your Skin Spell

This spell takes advantage of the energy of three creatures who change or freshen their appearance by literally coming out in a new skin: the cicada, the moth or butterfly, and the snake. And you're going to be using in this spell one of three things: the shed skin of a snake, the open and empty cocoon of a moth or butterfly, or the abandoned skin of a cicada.

Shudder now and get over the 'ick' factor- real magic requires girding up your loins and getting your hands dirty once in a while- as the gray witch will tell you.

Day: Friday- associated with Venus, beauty, and love
Hour: 1st/8th hour after sunrise;
3rd/10th hour after sunset
Planet: Venus
Moon Phase: waxing to full
Color: pink, white, silver,
Herbs: for beauty- ginseng, lilac, rose; for youth- catnip, valerian
Oil: rose oil
Stone: rose quartz
Number: 6
Letters: F, O, X- (no pun intended)
Symbols: The symbol for Venus
Deities: Venus/Aphrodite or Hathor

Items needed:
1. The dried shell of a cicada, a snakeskin, or abandoned cocoon
2. A fireproof bowl
3. A bottle of rose oil
4. A pink or white candle
5. A red flannel bag

This spell works on the refreshing metamorphic energy of the creatures listed here. It also works on the mind and what you see, or what you think you see. This spell is not an instant facelift, but rather, it changes the perception of how others view you and how you view yourself. It will give you the illusion of beauty and youth.

After the basic preparations are in place, the candles lit, the incense going, place upon your altar the fireproof bowl. Drop within it the insect skin, cocoon, or the snake shed and light it afire- you may need a bit of a flammable oil sprinkled on the top to get it going.

When the fire has gone out and the remains have cooled off a bit, using your pestle, crush what's left into a pulp, adding a few drops of rose oil and drippings from your pink or white candle until you get a good consistency with a nice scent. Now take it in your hands- yes, in your hands- and roll it into a ball...drop this treasure in the red flannel bag.

Keep this bag in a secret spot, and on the evening of a full moon bring it out when you are alone in a darkened candle-lit room. Stand before a mirror, calling to the changing energy of the creature whose remains are in the bag. Wave the bag in a gentle back and forth motion before your face, saying:

"By the power of the creature here,
May youth and beauty shine pure and clear.
By the power of the creature within,
May I shed what's old to reveal fresh young skin."

BANISHING SPELLS.
1. Basic Candle Spell and Correspondences
Day: Tuesday
Hour: 1st/8th hour after sunrise; 3rd/10th hour after sunset
Planet: Mars
Moon Phase: waning/dark
Color: red, orange, black

Herbs: dragon's blood, yarrow (arrowroot), cloves, St. John's Wort
Oils/Potions/Powder: Banishing Powder, Mars Astrological Oil
Incense: patchouli
Number: 9
Letters: I, R
Symbols: Mars, an image of the person/thing you wish to banish

Whether it's an individual or a set of circumstances that you wish to banish from your life, you can use the correspondences above to dress a spell candle and craft your magic. If it's a person you wish to be rid of, use their image, signature or a name paper to burn in your spell candle. If it's a set of circumstances you wish to banish, write out on a sheet of paper exactly what it is you want to go, and burn this paper in the flame of your dressed candle.

When this spell is complete, you will want to be rid of the remnants as soon as possible, and you will want them deposited as far from you and your home as is practical. The idea is that you are sending something 'away', and so highlight this fact through the energy of your magic and the last action of this spell.

2. Ditch It Quick Spell

There's someone/something you want to be rid of- fast. You don't have time for long drawn out rituals, you don't have time to wait for the moon or the energy of any particular planets. It may seem impulsive, but something tells you to it's necessary for your own safety, well-being, or sanity.

Let's do it.

Add a large spoonful of Banishing Powder to a jar of Four Thieves Vinegar. To this bottle, you will also add a slip of paper with your target's name upon it, a photo, or a name paper. If it's a situation that you wish to banish, add a small slip of paper explaining what the situation is.

Shake up the bottle. Put it in a black cloth bag, and tie the bag up with a black cord, tying three knots in the cord. Hide this bag somewhere safe for three days, then remove it from its hiding place and bury it off your property.

COLTSFOOT WEALTH SPELL.
Items: The husk from an ear of corn, a dollar, a note on parchment, coltsoot

leaves and green string or ribbon.
Ritual: For wealth and prosperity for a year, take the husk from an ear of corn
and put a dollar bill along with a note written on parchment,
"Oh, dear god of luck,
money is like muck,
not good except it is spread.
Spread some here at___(write in your address).
Thanks be to thee. Amen."
Sign your name. Sprinkle the dollar bill and note with coltsfoot leaves. Roll the
husk up and tie together with green string or ribbon. Hang the token up above the
entryway with green cord. That husk should bring riches into your home or
business by the bushel.

TO OBTAIN MONEY

Items: Cauldron, silver coin, and water
Time: Full Moon

Ritual: Fill your cauldron half full of water and drop a silver coin into it. Position
the cauldron so that the light from the moon shines into the water. Gently sweep
your hands just above the surface, symbolically gathering the Moon's silver.

While doing this say...
"Lovely Lady of the Moon, bring to me your
wealth right soon. Fill my hands with silver
and gold. All you give, my purse can hold."
Repeat this three times. When finished, pour the water upon the earth.

A QUICK MONEY SPELL.

Items: Green candle, cinnamon oil, a bill, patchouli incense
Ritual: This spell requires good visualization. Take a green candle and anoint it
with cinnamon oil. Take the bill or write on a piece of paper the amount of a bill
you owe and who it is too. You will need a candle that can burn for 7 days. Place the
paper under the candle. Hold your hands over the candle and say:
"This candle burns to light the way
for the money I need to pay this bill
in a way that harms no one."
Light the candle and burn patchouli incense. Meditate for about 5 minutes as the
candle burns. Visualize yourself writing the check or purchasing the money order
for this bill and putting it in the mail. Burn the candle every day around the same

time for 7 days and 15 minutes at a time. Also, burn patchouli incense every day
too with the candle. On the last day, burn the paper with the flame from the
candle and let the candle burn completely out.

HOUSE SECURE SPELL.

Items: Athame
Time: Waning Moon, as close to New Moon as possible.
Ritual: Raise Athame in salute to the Goddess and God, asking their assistance in
your "house cleaning". Now, beginning at the front door, walk throughout your
home clockwise. At each window, door or another opening, make an invoking
pentagram with your Athame. You may chant:
"Lord and Lady of the day, keep all harm far away,
Set your guard ever near, let no evil enter here"
After you have gone through your entire living space, visualize the 3D outline of
your home being completely made of and sealed with white light.
Thank the Lady
and the lord for their aid.

PROTECTION BOTTLE SPELL.

Items: 1 bottle with cork, 1 cup salt, 3 cloves garlic, 9 bay leaves, 7 tbsp. dried
basil, 4 tbsp. dill seeds, 1 tbsp. Sage, 1 tbsp. Anise, 1 tbsp. black pepper, 1 tbsp.
fennel
Time: Morning of a sunny day

Ritual: Place the salt in a bowl and say:
"Salt that protects, protect my home and all within it"
Add the rest, one by one saying the same words. Mix together with your hands,
lending energy. Visualize your home as a shining, safe, secure place of sanctuary.
Put the mixture in the jar. Seal and say:
"Salt and herbs, 9 times 9
Guard now this home of mine"
Keep the jar in a safe place or as an ornament.

SPELL TO PROTECT PETS.

Items: Pet fur - red thread of silk - canister
Ritual: Take some fur of the cat (shed fur will do nicely). Tie the fur into a bunch
with some red thread (silk by preference, although cotton or even acrylic will do).
Invoke the blessing of your patron deity. Place consecrated fur into a canister
(the following is imperative!). The canister must be reflective on the outside, but
NOT on the inside. Seal the canister with red wax (just a dab will do) Place
canister next to pet's usual exit. Red is the colour of protection, silk is an
insulator, the reflective canister reflects malicious intent, the blessing is for
extra whammy to the spell.

TO MAKE BAD LUCK GO AWAY.

Items: Cauldron, a piece of paper

Time: At night
Ritual: light a small fire in a cauldron or what ever you have available to contain
the fire. Write on a piece of paper that is 3 inches x 3 inches, the words BAD
LUCK. Then write down any bad things you do not like in your life right now. Then
draw a big X across the paper with a black marker. While doing this you should be
thinking of how all these things are going to disappear from your life, never to
return! Place the paper in the fire and repeat the following words 3 times:
"Fire, fire burning bright
turn my darkness into light!
Take away my bad luck ill,
bring me nothing but goodwill.
Bad luck came and stayed too long,
be gone forever, be gone, be gone!
With this fire burning bright,
bring me good luck, bring me light!"
"SO MOTE IT BE!"

TO STOP SLANDER AND GOSSIP.

Items: Cauldron - A piece of paper
Time: By night time
Ritual: Light a small fire in a cauldron or whatever you have available to contain
the fire. Write on a piece of paper that is 3 inches' x 3 inches, the word Rumours
and the rumours that are being spread about you. Do not write the names of those

who are slandering you! You do not want to harm them and suffer the
consequences with karma! Be thinking of these lies going away never to return as
you draw an X with a dark marker across the paper. Toss the paper into the fire
and repeat the following words 3 times:
"Rumours, slander standing stout,
with this X, I cross you out
I toss their words into the fire,
all these lies no longer hire
All bad things were done and said,
leave my life, be gone be dead!

All the evil that they say,
make it all go away!
Rumours carry me no more,
be gone be dead, be no more!"
"SO MOTE IT BE!"

SPELL TO FIND A JOB.

Items: 1 green candle - 1 black candle - Small jar - Nutmeg - Good luck oil -
Banishing oil - Rune for good fortune - Stone - A piece of paper with your perfect
job described on it.
Time: Waxing Moon
Ritual: Cast the Circle, Invoke the Gods, and anoint the black candle with
banishing oil and light it while you visualize all your obstacles falling away, and say:

"Bad luck flees, obstacles fall,

My path is clear, Heed my call"
Anoint the green candle with luck oil and say:
"Good luck is mine and prosperity
Help me Great Ones, come to me
Opportunity and rewards I see
As I will, So mote it be"

Meditate on the job you want as you gaze into the candle's flame. Still in the
circle, fill your good luck jar with the herbs, stone, note and rune figure. Seal the
jar with this words:
"Earth-born stone of brilliant hue
hearken to my deep desire
amidst the candle's radiant fire
Herbs of luck, prosperity
heed my call and bring to me
a better job, a new opportunity
As I will, so mote it be!"
Shake the jar, seal it with a kiss and place it back on the Altar.
Ground and centre,
thank the God and Goddess and close the Circle.

Each morning after, hold the jar while saying:
"God and Goddess
Hear as I pray
Let good fortune come my way
send me luck, prosperity
in my job search,
So mote it be!"
Shake the jar a few times, seal it with a kiss and replace it on the Altar.

Well Being Spell:

When you have been sick but are beginning to feel better, this is a good spell to cast. It is energizing and will leave you feeling healthier than when you began. For periodic maintenance, you may want to use the spell twice a year.

Things you will need -1 white or pink image candle powdered rose petals push pin thumbtack Star Oil (see below) Carve your name, or that of the person for whom you are casting the spell, onto the candle. Anoint the candle with the oil and sprinkle with powdered rose petals. Raise energy and focus on general wellbeing as you charge the candle. Burn under the waxing moon, chanting: Earth, Air, Fire, Water Peace, Health, Joy, Laughter. Peak the energy and let it fly out to the universe. Let the candle burn completely. (If you use runes you may also carve Sigel, Flame, and Caduceus in the wax before anointing the candle with oil.)

How to make Star Oil:
1/4-ounce almond oil 10 drops lemon oil 7 drops jasmine oil 7 drops rosemary oil
17 drops chamomile oil 5 drops sandalwood oil

BESOM BLESSING RITUAL.

There are, of course, many besom blessing rituals in existence and this is one that is commonly used. There is no right way or wrong way – it's whatever works for you. So if this besom blessing ritual doesn't feel quite right don't be afraid to change it. If you have several besoms you wish to bless, they can all be done at the same time. There is no need to perform the ritual individually although there is nothing wrong in doing so.

The ritual should be carried out on the night of the full moon. Make yourself comfortable on the floor with all the items in front of you.

You will need:

A white candle,
Incense,
A small dish of water,
Some salt.

When you are ready:
Light the candle and incense.
- Breathe in deeply through your nose (as if you were meditating) and visualize grounding energy filling your body.
- Breathe out through your mouth ridding yourself of all negativity.
- Repeat this process until you are completely relaxed and grounded.
- Pass the besom through the incense smoke and say: With scented air light and free, I give you breath. Blessed be.
- Pass the besom (very quickly) through the candle flame (being careful not to set the besom on fire or burn yourself obviously) and say:
- With fire dancing wild and free, I give you passion.

MAGICAL NUMBERS.

Numbers can be used in ritual and magickal workings. Odd numbers are related to the Goddess, women, and receptive energy. Even numbers are related to the God, men, and protective energy.

1: The Universe. The one and the source of all.

2: The Goddess and the God. Perfect duality and balance. The physical and spiritual equally combined.

3: The Triple Goddess. The physical, mental and spiritual aspects of ourselves. The lunar phases.

4: The Elements. The directions and seasons.

5: The senses. The elements plus Akasha. The pentacle/pentagram.

7: The planets as known in ancient times. Magick, power, and protection.

8: The number of Sabbats. A number of the God.

9: A number of the Goddess.

13: The number of Esbats. A lucky number.

15: A lucky number.

21: The number of Sabbats and moons in the Wiccan year.

28: A number of the moon.

101: The number of fertility.

WAND CONSECRATION RITUAL.

There are quite a few different consecration rituals but this is the one that we usually recommend. There is no one right way, nor is there a wrong way, so feel free to adapt the ritual if you wish.

You will need a white candle for the consecration flame, water, pentacle, and incense. To consecrate the tool, the elementals may be used.
Cast your circle.

Pick up the wand, saying: "I have chosen this wand to assist me in my work."

Visualize the wand being cleared of any negativity.

Continue till the wand feels clear to you.

Now visualize positive energy flowing from you, down your arm and into the wand.

Visualize a strong white light flowing through your body to the tool. Feel it absorb the positive energies.

Point the wand towards the North, saying: "May the powers of the Earth cleanse and fill the wand I have chosen. "Touch it to the pentacle, saying:" In the names of the Goddess and God (use any names you wish), I bless and make sacred this wand, tool of my craft. I charge this wand by the element of Earth."

Point the wand to the East, saying: "May the powers of the Air cleanse and fill the wand I have chosen." Pass the wand through the smoke of the incense, saying: "In the names of the Goddess and God (use any names you wish), I bless and make sacred this wand, a tool of my craft. I charge this wand by the element Air."

Point the wand to the South, saying: "May the powers of Fire cleanse and fill the wand I have chosen." Pass the wand quickly (the besom itself is obviously flammable) over the candle flame saying: "In the names of the Goddess and God (using any names you wish), I bless and make sacred this wand, a tool of my craft. I charge this wand by the element Fire."

Point the wand to the West, saying: "May the powers of water cleanse and fill the wand I have chosen." Sprinkle the wand with a few drops of water, saying: "In the names of the Goddess and God (using any names), I bless and make sacred this wand, tool of my craft. I charge this wand by the element Water."

Then say: "This tool is now ready, being consecrated and charged to assist me in my work. So mote it be."

Perform other workings if you wish, then close the circle

Your wand has now been successfully consecrated and is ready to be put to work.

FAIRY POEMS.

Few folks have seen a Fairy,
But I found this one for you.
If you believe with all your might
She'll make your dreams come true.
~ Author unknown

The woods are full of fairies!
The trees are alive:
The river overflows with them.
See how they dip and dive!
What funny little fellows!
What dainty little dears!
They dance and leap, and prance and peep,
And utter fairy cheers!
~Author unknown

Two little clouds, one summer's day,
Went flying through the sky;
They went so fast they bumped their heads,
And both began to cry.
Old Father Sun looked out and said:
'Oh, never mind, my dears,
I'll send my little fairy folk
To dry your falling tears.'
One fairy came in violet,
And one wore indigo;
In blue, green, yellow, orange, red,

They made a pretty row.
They wiped the cloud tears all away,
And then from out the sky,
Upon a line the sunbeams made,
They hung their gowns to dry.
~ Author unknown

Believe in the Fairies
Who make dreams come true.
Believe in the wonder,
The stars and the moon.
Believe in the magic,
From Fairies above.
They dance on the flowers,
And sing songs of love.
And if you just believe,
And always stay true,
The Fairies will be there,
To watch over you!
~ Author unknown

And as the seasons come and go,
here's something you might like to know.
There are fairies everywhere: under bushes, in the air,
playing games just like you play, singing through their busy day.
So listen, touch, and look around - in the air and on the ground.
And if you watch all nature's things, you might just see a fairy's wing.
~ Author unknown

There are fairies in your garden,
And they're flying everywhere

Over trees and under leaves
And spinning in the air.
There are fairies in your garden,
And it's plain for all to see
So look into your garden now
And you'll see some just like me!
~ Author unknown

~ Where you believe there is magic ... you will find it! ~

THE DAY I MET THE GREEN MAN.

I was sitting in my room reading a book about the Green man when I started to fall asleep.
I began to dream that I was in a forest, loads of trees surrounded me. I decided to go for a walk to see if anybody was about when I heard a noise coming from a gathering of trees in front of me.
I carried on walking towards the noise, and to my surprise standing there was the green man playing the panpipes.
He spotted me and stopped playing, he called me over, I walked over to him.
'Hello, young man, what is your name?' asked the Green man.
'I'm Ben, nice to meet you, sir, I was just reading about you for art class, 'I smiled.
The Green man smiled back at me.
'I'm glad to hear that young man, I've lived a long life and I'm loved by many.'
'Can you teach me how to play the panpipes?' I asked.
'Of course, 'he replied and handed me the tiny wooden instrument.
I blew into it and out came a soft musical sound, it was magical.
'You're doing great Ben,' said the Green man.

I awoke with a smile on my face and was looking forward to learning more about the Green man.

SEA MAGIC.

My heart faints in me for the distant sea.
The roar of London is the roar of ire
The lion utters in his old desire
For Libya out of dim captivity.
The long bright silver of Cheapside I see,
Her gilded weathercocks on roof and spire
Exulting eastward in the western fire;
All things recall one heart-sick memory: -

Ever the rustle of the advancing foam,
The surges' desolate thunder, and the cry
As of some lone babe in the whispering sky;
Ever I peer into the restless gloom
To where a ship clad dim and loftily
Looms steadfast in the wonder of her home.

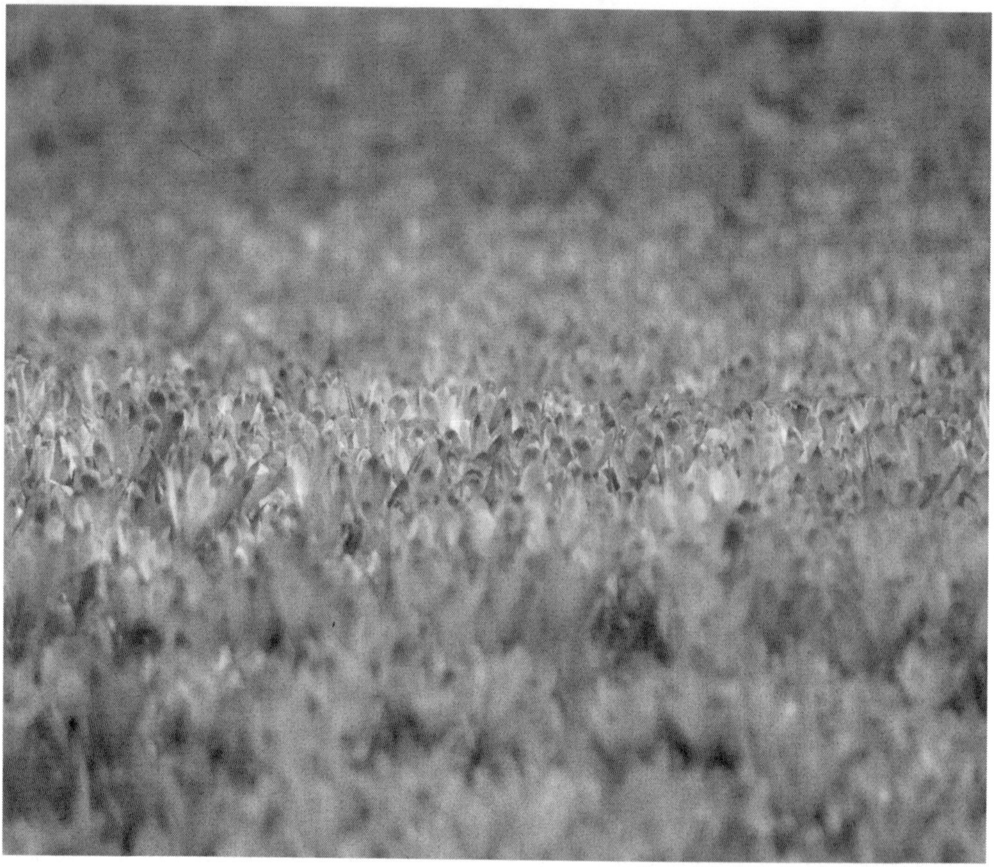

THANKYOU FOR READING THIS BOOK.
I HOPE YOU ENJOY IT AND LEARN A LOT OF NEW MAGICAL THINGS.
BLESSED BE
MYSTIC STORM